BUNNICULA

Deborah & James Howe

TEACHER GUIDE BY DORIS ROETTGER

About the Author

Dr. Doris Roettger is the Reading and Language Arts Coordinator for Heartland Area Education Agency in Des Moines, Iowa. A former elementary teacher, Title 1 reading teacher, reading consultant, and college professor, Dr. Roettger is an active member of the International Reading Association, a former Board member, and a member of the National Board for Professional Teaching Standards.

Product Manager:	Virginia Murphy
Editor:	Mary Jo Cosson
Cover and Book Design:	Randy Messer
Cover Illustration:	Paul Micich
Inside Illustration:	Randy Messer

Consulting Teachers

Katherine Backlund
Princeton, Minnesota

Christie Cochran
Vacaville, California

Lisa Craker
Traverse City, Michigan

Carol Fuhler
Crystal Lake, Illinois

Lee Hanzelon
West Des Moines, Iowa

Michael Higgins
Rothschild, Wisconsin

Alice Hudelson
Des Moines, Iowa

Dana Mason
Suburban, Maryland

Janet Morris
Bartow, Florida

Catherine Plaehn
Boyceville, Wisconsin

Beverly Plagge
Latimer, Iowa

Anne Power
Fremont, California

John Robbins
Rochester, New York

Peter Roop
Appleton, Wisconsin

Meredith Smith
Urbandale, Iowa

Bruce Solenski
Saratoga Springs, New York

Dr. Karen Spangenberg-Urbschat
Wayne, Michigan

Darlene Taylor-Bishop
Fairbanks, Alaska

Dawn Throlson
West Des Moines, Iowa

Madalyn VanderLinden
Indianola, Iowa

Toni Willett
Liberty, Missouri

Reading Beyond the Basal® Plus

If students are to become active readers, they need many opportunities to read the very finest in children's literature. Novels provide excellent opportunities for helping students deal with issues that are important to them and with which they can identify. Novels also introduce students to new ideas.

As students read, they often picture in their minds the events and characters described. The richness and depth of these pictures will be shaped by the experiences, thoughts, and feelings that the reader brings to the text.

Before-reading activities help students predict and think critically about key concepts and ideas they will encounter as they read a book—thus enhancing their understanding and making it easier for them to identify with the story and story characters.

Activities during reading help students reflect on what has happened in the story, think about what might have caused the events to happen, and anticipate and predict what might happen next.

Drama activities help students express their thoughts, values, and feelings while ''becoming'' the story characters—then stepping back and looking at the story from their own points of view. Through drama, students respond emotionally, physically, creatively, and intellectually to both situations and characters.

Discussion after reading enables students to share what they want to remember and how they feel about what happened in the story. Open-ended questions promote critical thinking, which deepens and enriches the students' understanding of the story and the issues presented. Discussion questions also strengthen the use of critical thinking skills, which need to be worked on every day.

Literary activities help students recognize the outstanding qualities of well-written literature. The activities in this guide encourage students to look at an author's style—how an author makes a story come to life, how he or she involves readers in the lives of the characters, and how he or she makes a reader respond to a story emotionally.

A novel's rich source of ideas helps students link reading and writing. Writing activities enhance students' personal responses to what they have read and help them sort out their feelings while relating to the story. The activities in this guide provide opportunities for students to make connections between the ideas in the book and their own lives.

The number of activities suggested in this *Reading Beyond the Basal® Plus* teacher guide enables you, the teacher, to decide which activities are most appropriate for your students. The activities may be used by cooperative learning groups or by individuals.

Activities are presented in sequential order for use before, during, and after reading the novel. However, most activities can be used whenever you feel they will be most instructive for your students.

The primary purpose of *Reading Beyond the Basal® Plus* is to provide ideas that will create thought-provoking and memorable experiences for your students as they become enthusiastic, thinking readers.

—Doris Roettger

Contents

The Story in Brief

"He's a bunny and we found him at a Dracula movie, so we'll call him Bunny-cula. Bun*nic*ula!''

And so it is that Bunnicula comes to live with Mr. and Mrs. Monroe, their sons, Toby and Pete, their cat, Chester, and their dog, Harold. Harold is the one who tells the story.

It seems Chester, a very well-read cat with a vivid imagination, is convinced that Bunnicula is a vampire bunny. Bunnicula's markings look like a black cape, he sleeps all day, and he doesn't eat his lettuce and carrots—instead, he drains their juices.

Then one night, Chester sees Bunnicula staring intensely toward some haunting violin music coming from a neighbor's. As Chester watches, Bunnicula smiles, showing, instead of a bunny's buck teeth—fangs! When all the vegetables in the kitchen turn white overnight, Chester's worst fears are confirmed.

Chester sets out to save the family by guarding Bunnicula's cage at night. Thus Bunnicula can't drain anything or *anyone*. But by saving the vegetables, Chester starves poor Bunnicula. In hopes of helping Bunnicula, Harold forms a plan to get the little rabbit some needed food. As a result of the chaos that follows, all three pets end up visiting the veterinarian.

In the end, Chester attends counseling sessions with a cat psychiatrist. The study of psychiatry opens up a whole new interest for him, and Chester soon forgets all about vampires.

Bunnicula is put on a diet of liquid carrots because of his near starvation. This, of course, suits Bunnicula just fine. Harold and Bunnicula become fast friends, often cuddling up by the fireplace for a friendly evening snooze.

The Monroe family changes grocery stores, assuming their vegetables were victims of some strange white blight!

Author! Author!

James Howe was born in 1946 in Oneida, New York. He majored in acting at Boston University. After graduating in 1968, he became a social worker in New York City. This change in vocational direction was a result of his conscientious objector status during the Vietnam War.

During this period, Howe married his first wife, Deborah, who was a writer and actress. Deborah Howe died of cancer in 1978.

After Howe's stint as a social worker, he returned to the theater as an actor and model, then as a director. But directing was not exactly what he wanted to do for a living, so Howe began a career as a writer.

Howe's writing career turned serious during graduate school at Hunter College when he attended a playwriting seminar and ended up writing two plays. During this same time, his wife Deborah suggested that she and her husband collaborate on a children's book based on a character James Howe had created several years earlier. The character was Count Bunnicula.

Describing the creation of *Bunnicula,* Howe recalls, "We sat around our kitchen table one night throwing ideas out to one another. It was in this session [that] we decided his victims would be vegetables, not people. It was truly a collaborative process. One of us would talk out loud while the other wrote frantically. As we inspired each other's thinking, the ideas and words overlapped until there were sentences, phrases even, that were truly the creation of two people."

After *Bunnicula,* the Howes together wrote *Teddy Bear's Scrapbook*. James Howe has gone on to write several more children's books since Deborah's death. Today he lives and works in New York City with his wife, Betsy Imershein, a theater producer.

About writing, Howe says, "I write for children because I like the child in myself. I find that when a so-called children's book is well-written, I can still enjoy reading it years later."

Setting the Stage for Reading

The following before-reading activities are intended to help students use their own experiences to better understand the concepts and ideas introduced in the story. Invite students to think critically about these issues and concepts and then share their ideas, feelings, and attitudes.

1. **Wild Imaginations**

   a. To help students remember what it was like to be afraid of the unknown when they were younger, read aloud the book *Bedtime for Frances* by Russell Hoban. In the story, Frances imagines all sorts of scary things before finally falling asleep at bedtime. Or read aloud the story *Buttermilk* by Stephen Cosgrove. In this story, a bunny learns what seems scary at night often turns out to be quite ordinary in the light of day.

   b. Ask students to remember a time when they saw or heard something that scared them, but that turned out to actually be something quite ordinary. Give students a few minutes to think of a scary time. Write the following sentence starters on the chalkboard. Have students complete the sentences in their journals (explained on page 15).

   > I was scared once when _____ .
   >
   > But it was only _____ .

c. Arrange students into small groups. Encourage students to describe to their groups what they heard or saw in such a way that the listeners can sense the fear that was felt at the time. Then have students tell what the object they heard or saw really was. Ask students to explain how they felt once they were no longer frightened.

d. Discuss reasons why people become afraid and what they might do to ease their fears in certain situations.

2. Vampires—Are They Real?

Ask students to name all the things they have ever heard or seen about vampires. Students might enjoy researching vampire bats, too. Compile a class list of vampire trivia for a bulletin-board display. Have students write interesting legends and facts on vampire- or bat-shaped paper.

3. Getting into the Book

a. Have students read the Editor's Note in the novel on pages xi and xii. Page numbers are provided for the Avon Camelot edition of the book. Begin a list of facts the class knows about the story from reading these two pages. Ask students why they think the author included an Editor's Note at the beginning of the story.

b. Discuss what the word *Bunnicula* might mean.

c. Have students read the Table of Contents and look at the pictures throughout the novel. Ask students what else they now think they know about the story. Add this information to the list.

d. Ask students to jot down questions in their journals that they would like answered by the time they finish reading the story. Compile a class list of questions about Bunnicula. Post the list for all to see. Encourage students to try to answer these questions in their journals as they read.

e. Have students predict in their journals what events might take place in the story.

4. **Rabbits As Pets**

"Adopt" a rabbit to keep in the classroom while students are reading the novel *Bunnicula*. A student in the school might have a pet rabbit that he or she is willing to "lend." Other sources for borrowing a rabbit would be a local 4-H member who keeps rabbits (contact the county conservation commission or the state fair board for names), a local science center, or a veterinarian.

As Students Read

As students read the novel *Bunnicula,* encourage them to keep a journal of their thoughts and feelings or participate in frequent group discussion. The following strategies provide opportunities for students to ask questions, clarify what they don't understand, react to what has happened, or predict what might happen next.

1. **Keeping a Personal Response Journal**

   a. A personal response journal is an effective way of getting students to record their thoughts and feelings as they read. Encourage students to write in their journals their reactions to important events and passages in the story. Students need to feel that the journal is truly theirs and that only they can share the contents of their journals with others.

   b. Explain to students that a journal is not a book report, but rather a list or notes of personal reflections. Encourage students to respond in their journals in a way that feels comfortable for them. If students have not kept a journal before, read the first chapter of the novel aloud, model the thought processes involved, and then write your reactions or feelings on the chalkboard or on chart paper as you would if you were writing in a journal. Consider keeping a journal, too, as a model for the students.

   c. Ask students to date each journal entry and note the page in the book where they have stopped reading to respond.

d. Here are some ideas for keeping a journal.

- Have students jot down the conclusions Chester makes about Bunnicula. Ask students to state whether they agree or disagree with Chester.

- Encourage students to record their own thoughts and questions about the story and story characters.

- Suggest that students record how Bunnicula might feel about various situations. Ask students to write some journal entries from Chester's point of view, too.

- Students might draw sketches or cartoons of favorite scenes from the story, using captions and balloons for dialogue.

2. **Reflecting and Anticipating**

The questions listed below can be useful in helping students reflect on what they have read, describe mental pictures they are forming as they are reading, or predict what might happen next in the story. The questions can be discussed with the class as a whole or in small groups. Students may be reading at different places in the book, yet all can still contribute.

- What is happening where you are reading now?

- How would you describe the characters so far?

- How accurate do you think Chester's observations are?

- Do you think Chester will be able to convince the Monroe family that Bunnicula is dangerous?

- What do you think will happen next? Why?

- How do you think this story will end?

Exploring the Use of Language

The following strategies can be used to help students determine the meanings of unfamiliar words or phrases they encounter in the novel *Bunnicula*. Teachers have the option of presenting an activity before students read the novel, as they read, or as an after-reading activity.

1. **Demonstrating Words**

   a. Write each of the following words or phrases on a large card. Make several card sets.

sauntered (page xi)	cat nap (page 44)
bounded (page 4)	scamper (page 50)
bereaved (page 9)	grimace (page 56)
moseyed (page 9)	lunged (page 59)
peered (page 14)	immerse (page 76)
made a beeline (page 16)	exemplary (page 78)
bleary-eyed (page 25)	petrified (page 89)

   b. Choose a word or phrase and model the process for finding the meaning of this word or phrase for students—look at the card with the particular word or phrase on it, then look the word up in the story. If meaning cannot be derived by looking at the story context, look the word up in a dictionary.

   c. Choose another word and model this same process for the students without telling them the word or its meaning. Then act out the word for students. Have students guess the word being demonstrated. When students have guessed the word, show the appropriate word card.

d. Arrange the class into groups of four or five students. Give each group a set of vocabulary cards. Have students select a card and then act out the meaning of the word or phrase for their group members. Encourage other students in the group to guess what the particular word or phrase is. This activity can be repeated several times so that all students can participate.

e. After the words have been sufficiently demonstrated, post the word cards in a convenient location in the classroom. Encourage students to use the new words daily in their speaking and writing.

f. These and other words and phrases in *Bunnicula* are also excellent for possible artwork activities. Suggest that students make an illustrated dictionary for use by future readers of *Bunnicula*. The dictionary could be bound and laminated, too.

2. **Self-Selected Vocabulary**

   a. Have students nominate outstanding or unusual vocabulary words from the novel *Bunnicula*. Write these words on the chalkboard, along with the number of the page on which each word appears in the novel. Have the student who nominates each word give the story context and then state why the word would be interesting or useful for the class to learn.

   b. Have all students look up the nominated word in the story and then read the surrounding paragraphs. Point out the clues in the sentence or paragraph that help students determine the meaning of the word. Have the group come to an agreed-upon meaning for the word in question. Write the definition on the chalkboard.

c. Compare the group definition of the word with the dictionary definition. Make any changes to the group definition that would help refine the word's meaning.

d. After students have nominated and defined several words, have the class narrow the list to ten or twelve particularly interesting or appropriate words. Have students record these words and their definitions in their journals.

e. Post the new words on cards around the room. Some ideas to help students remember the new words are listed below.

- Use the words in your own speaking.

- Encourage students to use the words in their speaking and writing. Reward students for using the new words.

- Add the new words to a class spelling lesson.

- Have students choose partners and quiz each other briefly on the new words.

- Encourage students to draw pictures depicting the words and attach the drawings to the posted word cards.

Drama and Oral Language Activities

The following drama and oral language activities invite students to draw on their own feelings and experiences as they react to the story. Encourage students to take the role of the characters as they participate in the activities.

1. Role-Playing

Write each of the situations listed below on a large card. Arrange students into small groups. Have each group choose a card and role-play what *could* have happened during each episode. Before students begin role-playing, have them reread the pages listed. Ask students to imagine that just as Harold and Chester can talk, so can Bunnicula.

- Harold and Chester take Bunnicula out of his cage (second paragraph on page 70 through the seventh paragraph on page 73)

- Harold tries to talk with Bunnicula (third paragraph on page 79 to the bottom of page 80)

- Chester attempts to destroy the vampire in Bunnicula (pages 81 and 82)

- Harold takes Bunnicula out of the cage and puts him on the table to eat the salad (page 86 through the sixth paragraph on page 89)

- Bunnicula talks to Harold after his trip to the veterinarian (third paragraph on page 93)

- Bunnicula and Harold snuggle up by the fireplace while Harold sings Bunnicula a lullaby (tenth paragraph on page 95)

2. Readers' Theater

a. The conversations on the following pages are excellent for Readers' Theater.

- Bunnicula's arrival (pages 3 through 10)

- Naming Bunnicula (pages 10 through 17)

- The Monroes finding the white tomato (pages 32 through 36)

- The Monroes finding more white vegetables and Chester trying to tell the family about his suspicions (pages 53 through 61)

- Harold bringing Bunnicula to the dinner salad (pages 83 through 91)

b. Have students rewrite the script, eliminating all *said* phrases. Writers might incorporate suggestions for tone of voice in their scripts as well.

c. Ask students to read the various parts using their best dramatic reading voices. Remind students that all emotions in the story should be conveyed through the students' voices. Have students read several parts before they are assigned a role. After you and the students have agreed on the readers for the various roles, give the readers time to practice.

d. Have the narrators stand and the remainder of the readers sit on chairs facing the audience.

3. Using Persuasion

a. Have students look through the novel to find the episodes where Chester tried to persuade Harold and the family that Bunnicula was a vampire.

b. Have students brainstorm about times when they have tried to persuade someone. List the various methods of persuasion they used on the chalkboard. Some examples are bullying, using facts, reasoning, and appealing to the emotions.

c. Ask volunteers to choose one of the persuasive methods listed and then try to convince other students that Bunnicula is, indeed, a vampire bunny.

Developing Critical Thinking

The following questions encourage students to think critically about the characters, their behaviors, and what happens in the story. Questions might be discussed in a small group, or a panel could be arranged for students to take different sides on the various issues. Encourage students to go back into the book to find examples that support their opinions. Also, encourage examples from students' personal experiences.

1. How does Chester get his information to draw conclusions about Bunnicula? What evidence does Chester have that Bunnicula is a vampire? How valid are Chester's clues?

2. What incidents from the story make you think Chester has a very active imagination? How could an active imagination get you into trouble?

3. What do you think caused the vegetables to turn white? What information do you have to support your theory?

4. Do you think Harold agreed with Chester's ideas about Bunnicula? What did Harold do that leads you to this decision?

5. What rumors could be started from the incidents in this story? How might the rumors spread?

6. How do you think Bunnicula got in and out of his cage without Chester or Harold seeing him?

7. What parts of the story make Chester's conclusions seem believable? What parts of the story seem like make-believe?

8. How typical are Pete and Toby in the way each wanted Bunnicula to stay in his room? How do you think you would have behaved?

9. What clues does the author give to show that Harold and Chester are friends? Why do you think Harold and Chester are good friends? How did Harold happen to become friends with Bunnicula? How do you think Harold's friendship with Bunnicula affected his friendship with Chester?

10. On the last page of the story, Harold tells the reader to "draw your own conclusions" about Bunnicula. What conclusions do you draw about Bunnicula? Why?

Reading As a Writer

The following activities are designed to help students become aware of an author's style—the way an author makes the story come alive, how he or she guides the reader to know the story characters and their feelings, and the techniques an author uses to help the reader see how characters handle their various problems.

1. **Story in the First Person**

   a. Have students reread the first two pages of the novel to determine who is telling the story. Explain to students that when authors write as if the main character is telling the story, this is called writing in the first person. Help students become aware of the differences between stories written in the first person and stories written in the third person. Post the following in a prominent place in the classroom.

First Person	Third Person
Narrator uses the pronouns *I* or *we*	Narrator uses the pronouns *he*, *she*, or *they*
Story is told from a story character's point of view	Story is told from an outsider's point of view
Readers feel like they could be the storyteller	Readers know that the story is about someone else

b. Borrow enough novels from the school library so that each student has his or her own book. Read aloud a passage from a novel written in the first person and a passage from a novel written in the third person. Have students scan their novels to determine whether their novels are written in the first person or third person, then state their opinions and read a passage aloud to support their views.

c. Keep a classroom list of book titles written in the first and third persons. As students read new novels, have them add their novel titles to the appropriate lists.

2. Personification

a. Explain to students that personification is the giving of human characteristics to ideas, objects, or animals. Offer as examples some stories incorporating personification that all students would be familiar with, such as "The Three Bears," "Little Red Riding Hood," or "The Gingerbread Boy." Ask students to name other stories they know of that also use personification.

b. Arrange students into cooperative working groups of two or three students. Assign each group a chapter. Ask students to look through their chapters to determine how either Chester or Harold acts like a person. Have each group list their character's human characteristics on the reproducible provided on page 46. For fun, ask students to list any animal characteristics they think they might possess, too.

c. When the lists have been completed, have students compare their lists to determine whether Harold and Chester have similar human characteristics.

3. **The Use of Puns**

   a. Ask students to reread pages 71 through 73 in the novel to find out how Chester confused the words *stake* and *steak*. Help students understand the spelling and meaning of each word. Explain that when authors use words humorously to show more than one meaning, they are using a pun.

   b. Have the class begin a collection of puns. Some sources of puns are Howe's books *Howliday Inn* and *The Celery Stalks at Midnight*, the *Amelia Bedelia* books by Peggy Parish, *The King Who Rained* by Fred Gwynne, knock-knock jokes, homonym dictionaries, and some *Family Circus* cartoons. As students bring in examples, have them point out the puns and the different meanings of the words.

   c. Have students create a bulletin board of puns. Include students' drawings of puns, too.

4. **Developing a Bibliography**

   a. On page 19 in the novel, Harold states that Chester reads mystery stories and tales of horror and the supernatural. Have students develop a chart, entitled "Chester's Bibliography," that includes books from each category.

   b. Discuss how reading these scary books might have influenced Chester's thinking.

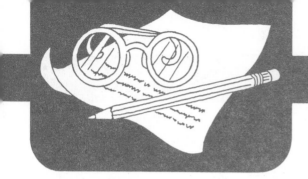

The Reading-Writing Connection

Ideas and events in a novel often spark exciting writing possibilities for students. Several activities that encourage student writing are provided in this section. Some of the suggestions are appropriate for students to complete as they are reading the novel. Others are more suitable as after-reading activities. Students may wish to choose one or more of the activities, or come up with additional writing ideas of their own.

Consider guiding students through the writing steps to be sure they fully understand the writing process. Students might not always complete all of the writing steps, however— sometimes the writing process might go no further than drafting and sharing. Other times the author may wish to carry the writing process through to publishing. Encourage listeners to make constructive, supportive comments during sharing.

1. **Writing the Story Before**

   a. *Prewriting.* Ask students to think about how the Monroe family happened to find Bunnicula. Have students consider different ways Bunnicula could have gotten into the movie theater.

   b. *Drafting.* Ask students to draft a short story about how Bunnicula arrived at the movie theater. Encourage students to follow the guidelines for writing a story provided on the next page.

   c. *Sharing.* Pair students to share the drafts of their stories. Encourage the listeners to praise the authors for something that is particularly good in each story. If the listeners have questions or would like to know more about a particular part of a story, they should ask the author to provide additional details.

Guidelines for Writing a Story

Setting

> Introduce the most important character(s).
> Describe the place and time.

Beginning

> Describe an event that sets up a problem for the
> main character.

Simple Reaction

> Describe the character's thoughts and feelings about
> the problem.

Goal

> Describe what the main character wants to do about
> the problem.

Attempt

> Describe how the main character tries to solve the
> problem.

Outcome

> Tell whether the attempts are successful or not.

Ending

> Wrap up the story. Tell any consequences.

d. *Revising.* Have authors revise their drafts to incorporate all or some of their partners' suggestions, if they wish.

e. *Editing.* Have the same partners read each other's stories for correct spelling, capitalization, and punctuation. Encourage partners to suggest any word changes they feel might improve the story, too.

f. *Publishing.* Ask students to design their own bunny-shaped books. Have students cut construction paper and lined paper from their bunny patterns and staple the sheets together. Have students copy their final drafts inside the bunny-shaped books and decorate the covers. The front cover could represent Bunnicula as everyone saw him. The back cover could represent Bunnicula as Chester saw him. Display the books in the classroom.

2. Describing a Scene from a Different Point of View

a. *Prewriting.* Ask students to reread the scene beginning on page 56 in the book and ending at the bottom of page 59 in which Chester attempts to warn the family that Bunnicula is dangerous. Arrange students into five groups—one group for each of the characters present—Dad, Mom, Toby, Pete, and Chester. Exclude Harold. Ask each group to describe what happened in the kitchen from the point of view of the group's character. Give the groups about ten minutes to practice their presentations.

b. *Drafting.* Ask students to write a description of the scene in the kitchen from the viewpoint of their character. Encourage students to use vivid adjectives and adverbs.

c. *Sharing.* Have students form groups consisting of one of each of the characters. As authors read their descriptions, ask the listeners to determine whether the authors have written from the viewpoints of their characters.

d. *Revising.* Ask the listeners to first tell the authors what they liked about the descriptions. Have listeners suggest any improvements they feel would be helpful. The authors should then decide which suggestions they will incorporate into their revised descriptions.

e. *Editing.* Have authors work with partners to edit the final drafts for correct spelling, capitalization, and punctuation.

f. *Publishing.* Create a point-of-view bulletin board or interest center. Group descriptions by character so that students can see the various points of view. Students might enjoy drawing or painting cutouts of the five characters to make the display more eye-catching.

3. **Creating a Memorable Character**

a. *Prewriting.* On page 57 in the novel, Mr. Monroe says, ''All cats are as individual as all people.'' Ask students what this phrase means. Explain to students that authors create memorable characters by giving them unique traits, such as odd eating habits. Ask students to recall Harold's, Chester's, or Bunnicula's peculiar traits. Bring in comic strips or books about Garfield, Snoopy, Marmaduke, or other popular cartoon characters. Have students list the special traits the cartoonists have given each of these characters. Ask students to imagine a unique character and give this character some surprising traits. Suggest that students describe how the character looks and what he or she likes to do.

b. *Drafting*. Ask students to write about their unique characters for their classmates. Have students introduce their characters in the first paragraph. Then have students create an episode that shows their characters in action.

c. *Sharing*. Have students form small groups. Encourage authors to ask the listeners for specific comments, such as

  • Do the words I use help you see my character in your imagination? Tell me what you see.

  • Does my scene show you what my character is like?

  • What more would you like to know?

d. *Revising*. First, ask listeners to share with the author at least one thing they especially liked about the character description. Ask the listeners to provide constructive comments on what the author has asked for. It may be helpful to model giving thoughtful, constructive criticism for the students.

e. *Editing*. Have authors choose a partner and then read their descriptions aloud. Partners might suggest adverbs or adjectives to help make the paragraphs even more descriptive.

f. *Publishing*. Suggest that students portray their descriptions using various media—from cartoons to three-dimensional representations, such as stuffed animals or creatures made from boxes, tubes, or stuffed hosiery. Post all completed descriptions on a bulletin board or place descriptions in a folder for students to read during free time. Display the character portrayals in the classroom, too.

Across-the-Curriculum Activities

The following activities are designed to incorporate literature across the curriculum. Teachers have the option of presenting an activity as students read the novel or as an after-reading activity.

1. **Health**

   a. Begin a unit on nutrition by having students reread page 37 in the novel, which describes the foods Harold enjoys on Friday nights. Ask students to list their own favorite foods for snacks, breakfast, lunch, and dinner on the reproducible provided on page 47.

   b. Have students find out the number of servings from each of the four basic food groups that should be in their daily diet.

   c. Invite a representative from the school district's food service to come speak to the class about the government guidelines that school food services must follow in providing a balanced meal. Seek permission from the food service for the class to plan a school lunch menu.

   d. Write a group letter to the school cooks thanking them for their cooperation in the lunch project. Encourage students to compliment the cooks on the foods prepared—especially their favorite foods.

   e. As an alternate activity, study only snack foods. Have students examine the ingredients in their favorite snacks. Make a list of nutritious snacks. Encourage students to bring healthy snacks to school to share on a special wholesome snack-food day.

2. Science

a. Ask students to reread the family's discussion on pages 54 and 55 in the novel about the vegetables turning white. Have students place a stalk of celery in a glass filled with colored water. In about an hour, the leaves and stem should be streaked with color. Students can look at the ends of the celery stalks to see the tubes that have conducted the color up the stalks. Students might try dyeing cauliflower, radishes, potatoes, and other light-colored vegetables, too.

b. Have students contact the state department of agriculture, requesting information on the effects of herbicides and pesticides on vegetables. Encourage students to read the information and prepare oral reports for the class.

3. Social Studies

Harold states that the note found on Bunnicula was written in an obscure dialect of the Carpathian Mountain region in Transylvania. On a map of Europe, help students locate Transylvania in Romania. Encourage students to read about Transylvania in an encyclopedia or other library sources.

4. Music

a. On page 23 in the novel, Chester and Bunnicula listen to their neighbor, Professor Mickelwhite, play a haunting melody on his violin. Arrange for the students to listen to some haunting violin music as they read the novel. One selection which may be appropriate is the recording "Traditions" by Itzhak Perlman (with the Israeli Philharmonic Orchestra).

b. Students might pretend to be Bunnicula as they listen to the violin music, too. Ask students to very slowly change their own facial expressions to what they imagine a vampire would look like. As students continue to listen to the music, ask them to continue to change their expressions to fit the mood.

5. **Art**

Explain to students that a caricature is a drawing of someone or something that is exaggerated by distorting certain features. If possible, show students a caricature of a well-known person (political cartoonists often draw caricatures). List descriptive words and phrases about Bunnicula on the chalkboard. Encourage students to use their imaginations to draw interesting caricatures of Bunnicula showing how he looked to Chester. Some students might want to draw how they think Chester looked to Bunnicula, too.

Just-for-Fun Activities

The following activities are based on ideas presented in the novel and are intended just for fun.

1. a. Mrs. Monroe came up with the name Bunnicula by combining the words bunny and Dracula. Encourage students to combine other words to form a new word, too. Keep a list of the students' ideas.

   b. Discuss how and why students came to name their own pets.

2. Have small groups of students create large papier-mâché rabbits. Have students use a round balloon for the head and a round or oblong balloon for the body. Wire can be used to form the ears and feet. Some students might decorate their rabbits to resemble Bunnicula as everyone saw him. Other students might decorate their rabbits to resemble Bunnicula as Chester saw him.

3. To help students understand that things are not always as they seem, demonstrate how to make shadow animals with your hands. Directions for making some shadow animals are provided on page 48.

4. a. On page 39 in the story, Toby tells Harold about the book *Treasure Island*. To Harold, chocolate cake was a treasure. Post a large sheet of butcher paper cut in the shape of a treasure chest. Have students write or draw what they consider to be their own personal treasures.

b. Sponsor a personal treasure day. Have students bring in and share a possession with the class that they consider to be valuable.

5. a. Hold a trial for Bunnicula. Have students volunteer for the roles of judge, prosecuting attorney, defense attorney, jury members, witnesses, and the defendant. Have the attorneys prepare evidence and interview witnesses before the trial begins.

   b. Invite an attorney or judge to come speak to the class about the judicial process and to answer questions the students might have as they prepare for the trial.

6. Ask students to imagine that they are looking for a pet. Have students jot down qualities that they would look for. Then have students compare their lists. Make a class chart to show which qualities in a pet are considered to be the most important.

7. Have students imagine that they are a pet advertising for a new owner. What qualifications would they want their owner to possess? Have students draft an ad for a home from the pet's point of view. Before students begin writing, have them read ads in a local newspaper to gain an understanding of the type of language that is often used in advertising.

8. Chester is embarrassed when he has to wear his bright yellow sweater decorated with purple mice in cowboy hats. Hold a just-for-fun "embarrassing day" where everyone wears or brings in to share something that would normally embarrass him or her.

9. a. On page 8 in the story, Harold says " . . . most people might call me a mongrel, but I have some pretty fancy bloodlines running through these veins and Russian wolfhound happens to be one of them." Encourage students to investigate dog breeds and prepare a chart or oral report to present to the class.

   b. Invite a veterinarian or breeder to come talk to the class about the various breeds of dogs.

10. On page 19 in the novel, Harold explains that he found *Jonathan Livingston Seagull* by Richard Bach particularly delicious. On page 20, Chester is reading Edgar Allan Poe's "The Fall of the House of Usher." And on page 39, Toby is reading *Treasure Island* by Robert Louis Stevenson. Choose one of these stories as a read-aloud treat for the class to enjoy as well.

An Annotated Bibliography

Listed here are some books about animals personified and other fantasies that would be of interest to students who enjoyed *Bunnicula,* as well as additional books by Deborah and James Howe. The letters *RL* in the brackets indicate the reading level of the book listed. *IL* indicates the approximate interest level.

- **Babe, the Gallant Pig** by Dick King-Smith. When Babe arrives in the farmyard, the farmer's wife immediately thinks of bacon. Fly the sheepdog recognizes Babe as a nuisance, but when she adopts the motherless piglet, she is surprised at how quickly Babe learns. Dell, 1987. [RL 5.8 IL 4-7]

- **Babes in Toyland** by James Howe. Based on the 1903 operetta, Jane and Alan survive a shipwreck arranged by their devious, miserly Uncle Barnaby, who seeks to inherit their fortunes. The youngsters escape to toyland where they outwit their uncle and, at the same time, rid toyland of an evil toymaker. Harcourt, Brace, Jovanovich, 1986. [RL 6 IL 3+]

- **Bats on the Bedstead** by Norma Tadlock Johnson. Moving a thousand miles away from his old school and friends is tough enough on eleven-year-old Ricky without the added pressure of a new house possessed by bats who want Ricky and his family to move. Houghton Mifflin, 1987. [RL 4.6 IL 3-7]

- **Ben and Me** by Robert Lawson. The life and times of Benjamin Franklin are delightfully narrated by his good friend and cohort, Amos the mouse. Dell, 1973. [RL 7.3 IL 3-7]

- **The Cat Who Went to Heaven** by Elizabeth Coatsworth. A little cat and a compassionate Japanese artist bring about a miracle. Macmillan, 1967. [RL 6 IL 4-6]

- **The Celery Stalks at Midnight** by James Howe. Chester the cat is more convinced than ever that Bunnicula is a vampire bunny, especially when a trail of white vegetables is found the morning after the rabbit disappears. En route to finding Bunnicula and hence, they think, to saving the town, Chester, Harold, and Howie experience a wild array of adventures. Atheneum, 1983. [RL 5 IL 3-7]

- **Charlotte's Web** by E. B. White. Wilbur, a lovable pig, is rescued from a cruel fate by a beautiful and intelligent spider named Charlotte. Harper and Row, 1952. [RL 5 IL 3-6]

- **The Dancing Cats of Applesap** by Janet Taylor Lisle. Melba, a very shy ten-year-old, comes every day to be served a hot fudge sundae in Mr. Jiggs' failing old-fashioned drugstore—in which 100 wondrous dancing cats live. Bantam Books, 1985. [RL 5 IL 4+]

- **Eat Your Poison, Dear** by James Howe. The third Sebastian Barth mystery features a crime everyone will relate to—someone is poisoning the cafeteria food at Pembroke Middle School. Atheneum, 1986. [RL 5 IL 5-8]

- **The Enormous Egg** by Oliver Butterworth. Twelve-year-old Nate Twitchell never had much excitement in his life—until one of his hens lays an egg the size of a melon and the creature that hatches makes world news. Dell, 1987. [RL 5.7 IL 3-7]

- **Fantastic Mr. Fox** by Roald Dahl. Mr. Fox, a truly fantastic fellow, outwits three rich, mean farmers who are determined to catch him. Alfred A. Knopf, 1986. [RL 3.3 IL 3-6]

- **Harry Cat's Pet Puppy** by George Selden. Tucker Mouse and Harry Cat of *The Cricket in Times Square* take on the responsibility of raising a bedraggled puppy abandoned in an alley. Farrar, Straus and Giroux, 1974. [RL 6.1 IL 4-6]

- **Howliday Inn** by James Howe. While investigating the horrible howling which emanates from Chateau Bow Wow, Chester and Harold stumble on a mystery involving some suspicious disappearances—and maybe murder. Avon Books, 1974. [RL 4 IL 3-7]

- **James and the Giant Peach** by Roald Dahl. James sadly resigns himself to a life of continued misery with his two wicked aunts after he drops a bag of magic, given to him by a strange little man, under the old peach tree—until he notices an amazing peach starting to grow at the top of the tree. Bantam Books, 1984. [RL 4 IL 4-7]

- **Morgan's Zoo** by James Howe. The city is going to shut down the Chelsea Park Zoo—but twins Allison and Andrew, zookeeper Morgan, and the animals all save the day. Avon Books, 1986. [RL 5.5 IL 3-7]

- **Mrs. Frisby and the Rats of NIMH** by Robert O'Brien. A widowed mouse, Mrs. Frisby, attempts to save her family by acquiring some help from the well-taught rats of NIMH. Macmillan, 1971. [RL 6 IL 3-7]

- **The Muppet Guide to Magnificent Manners** by James Howe. Kermit explains proper introductions, conversations, thank-you notes, table manners, and other mannerly matters. Random House, 1984. [RL 6.1 IL 3-7]

- **Mystery Cat** by Susan Saunders. He's got nine lives, a sixth sense for trouble, and he's always where the action is. Mystery Cat—by day he belongs to Kelly Ann McCoy, by night he's the pet of Hillary Barnett. In truth, nobody owns M.C.—and what's more, he's the cat who has a handle on every crime in Windsor! Bantam Books, 1986. [RL 4 IL 3 +]

- **A Night Without Stars** by James Howe. Frightened by the prospect of open-heart surgery and unable to get answers to her questions from the hospital staff or her family, eleven-year-old Maria finds strength through her friendship with an embittered, scarred burn victim. Avon Books, 1985. [RL 5.4 IL 5 +]

- **Nighty-Nightmare** by James Howe. This fourth installment of the adventures of Bunnicula, Harold the dog, Chester the cat, and Howie the new pup, reveals the chilling history of the notorious vampire bunny after Chester, Harold, and Howie are lost in the woods during a camping trip. Macmillan, 1987. [RL 5.2 IL 3-7]

- **Owls in the Family** by Farley Mowat. Owls Wol and Weeps turn a household upside down, outwit a dog, and shake up a neighborhood. Bantam Books, 1981. [RL 4 IL 4 +]

- **The Pet of Frankenstein** by Mel Gilden. Hoping to impress his dad with his scientific savvy, Frankie Stein decides to reconstruct the pet dog of his great-granduncle (once-removed), the Baron Victor Frankenstein. Avon Books, 1988. [RL 5.4 IL 3-7]

- **Quentin Corn** by Mary Stolz. When he learns his owner is planning to eat him, Quentin the pig steals some clothes and disguises himself as a boy. He gets a job as a handyman's helper, finds a room in a boardinghouse, and makes friends with a little girl named Emily. Dell, 1988. [RL 6.4 IL 4-7]

- **Rabbit Hill** by Robert Lawson. The story of Father and Mother Rabbit, their high-leaping son, Little Georgie, aged Uncle Analdas, and a host of other animals. Viking, 1944. [RL 6.6 IL 4-8]

- **Socks** by Beverly Cleary. A comfortable cat's life for Socks is disrupted by the arrival of a new baby in his owner's family. Dell, 1980. [RL 5.8 IL 3-7]

- **Stage Fright** by James Howe. Thirteen-year-old Sebastian Barth and his friends uncover the truth behind the frightening events that threaten the life of movie star Michaele Caraway and a summer stock company. Avon Books, 1987. [RL 4.8 IL 5 +]

- **Teddy Bear's Scrapbook** by Deborah and James Howe. On a rainy day when there's nothing to do, Teddy Bear brings out his scrapbook that chronicles his adventures as a cowboy, great explorer, circus performer, ace reporter, movie star, and best friend. Atheneum, 1980. [RL 4.3 IL 2-6]

- **The Trouble with Tuck** by Theodore Taylor. Based on a true story, a young girl works against all odds to provide her blind dog with a guide dog of his own. Avon Books, 1983. [RL 4 IL 5 +]

- **The Trumpet of the Swan** by E. B. White. Louis the Trumpeter Swan has no voice with which to communicate, so he learns to read and write, and to play the trumpet, too. Harper and Row, 1973. [RL 5 IL 3-8]

- **Tucker's Countryside** by George Selden. Tucker Mouse and Harry Cat respond to an urgent call for help from their Connecticut friend, Chester Cricket. Farrar, Straus and Giroux, 1969. [RL 6 IL 3-7]

- **What Eric Knew** by James Howe. Things are pretty dull in Pembroke, Connecticut, after the adventuresome Eric Mather moves away. When Sebastian starts receiving notes from Eric, he finds himself right in the middle of an intriguing mystery involving drugs, an ancient murder, and a ghost. Macmillan, 1985. [RL 4.6 IL 5+]

- **The Wind in the Willows** by Kenneth Grahame. Told through the voices of Mole, Toad, Water Rat, and Badger, the reader experiences the river, the wild wood, and what it's like to take to the open road. Scribners, 1961. [RL 5 IL 3+]

- **Witch-Cat** by Joan Carris. Gwen Markham has just learned that she's a witch! Now it's up to Rosetta, the witch-cat, to teach her to understand and use her new-found powers, but science buff Gwen proves to be a handful. Dell, 1986. [RL 5.1 IL 5+]

- **The Witches of Worm** by Zilpha Keatley Snyder. Jessica, a twelve-year-old with a difficult home life, finds an ugly kitten that she names ''Worm.'' It's not long before Jessica imagines that her cat has the power to bewitch her. Atheneum, 1972. [RL 5.6 IL 4-7]

Personification of _____

Directions: List Chester or Harold's human characteristics. Include the page number on which the characteristic is described.

Page   Human Characteristic

____   _____

____   _____

____   _____

____   _____

____   _____

____   _____

____   _____

____   _____

____   _____

____   _____

____   _____

Now turn the question around. What animal characteristics do you possess? What animal would you want to be? Why?

Name   Animal

_____   _____

_____   _____

46

Favorite Foods

Directions:

1. List a favorite food for snack, breakfast, lunch, and dinner.

2. Check the food group to which each favorite food belongs. If a food belongs in more than one category, check each appropriate category.

3. Look over the categories you have checked. How well do your favorite foods contribute to a balanced diet?

Food Groups

	Meats	Grains	Dairy	Fruits and Vegetables	Other
Snack					
Breakfast					
Lunch					
Dinner					

47

Shadow Animals

Directions: Hold your hands in the following shapes in front of a projector shining against a screen or light-colored wall.

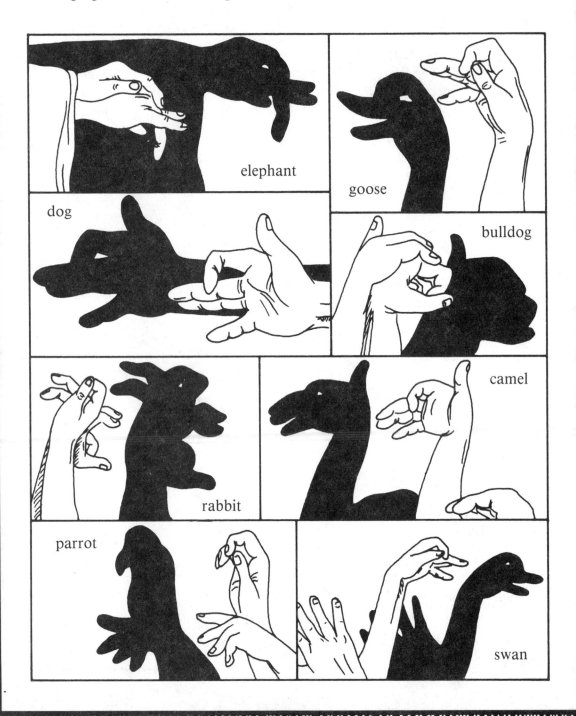

elephant

goose

dog

bulldog

rabbit

camel

parrot

swan